EDGE
BOOKS™

WILD MOMENTs IN STOCK-CAR RACING

BY M WEBER

D1144393

Raintree is an imprint of Capstone Global Library Limited, a company incorporated in England and Wales having its registered office at 264 Banbury Road, Oxford, OX2 7DY – Registered company number: 6695582

www.raintree.co.uk
myorders@raintree.co.uk

Text © Capstone Global Library Limited 2018
The moral rights of the proprietor have been asserted.

All rights reserved. No part of this publication may be reproduced in any form or by any means (including photocopying or storing it in any medium by electronic means and whether or not transiently or incidentally to some other use of this publication) without the written permission of the copyright owner, except in accordance with the provisions of the Copyright, Designs and Patents Act 1988 or under the terms of a licence issued by the Copyright Licensing Agency, Saffron House, 6–10 Kirby Street, London EC1N 8TS (www.cla.co.uk). Applications for the copyright owner's written permission should be addressed to the publisher.
Printed and bound in China.

Editorial Credits
Lauren Dupuis-Perez, editor; Sara Radka, designer; Laura Manthe, production specialist

ISBN 978-1-4747-4496-6 (paperback)
22 21 20 19 18 17
10 9 8 7 6 5 4 3 2 1

British Library Cataloguing in Publication Data
A full catalogue record for this book is available from the British Library.

Quote Sources
p.6, "Historical Motorsports Stories: Details of Largest Crash in NASCAR History." Racing Reference, racing-reference.info, February 18, 2016; p.15, "1987 Winston: Elliott Will 'Never Forget' Earnhardt's All-Star Move." nascar.com, May 17, 2016; p.25, "Kurt Busch Recalls Infamous Busch Bros. All-Star Wreck." SBNation. com, May 21, 2010; p.28, "VIDEO: Stock Car Champ Walks Away from Spectacular Cowdenbeath Shunt." www. thecourier.co.uk, May 29, 2016

Acknowledgements
AP Images: Associated Press, 9; Getty Images: ISC Archives, 10, 13, Getty Images: 21; Newscom: 8, 27, Brian Cleary/Icon SMI, 14, 18, 23, David Allio/Icon SMI, 8, 17, Jeff Corder/Icon SMI, 25, Malcolm Hope/ Icon Sportswire, 5, MCT, 26, UPI, 15, Walter G Arce/Icon SMI 285, cover, ZUMAPRESS/Arthur Grace, 19, ZUMAPRESS/Tony Marshall/PA Wire, 29; Shutterstock: Action Sports Photography, 7; graphic elements by Book Buddy Media

The publisher does not endorse products whose logos may appear on objects in images in this book.

Every effort has been made to contact copyright holders of material reproduced in this book. Any omissions will be rectified in subsequent printings if notice is given to the publisher.

All the Internet addresses (URLs) given in this book were valid at the time of going to press. However, due to the dynamic nature of the Internet, some addresses may have changed, or sites may have changed or ceased to exist since publication. While the author and publisher regret any inconvenience this may cause readers, no responsibility for any such changes can be accepted by either the author or the publisher.

CONTENTS

STOCK-CAR RACING

Stock-car racing is one of the most exciting motor sports in the world. Stock-cars are based on production models of regular cars. But underneath the bonnet these cars are built for speed.

In the United States the National Association for Stock Car Racing (NASCAR) organizes this popular sport. Huge crowds attend NASCAR races all over the country. Stock-cars also race in different places around the world.

It is a competition where every second counts. Drivers must fight to stay ahead. When cars collide, or a driver loses control, it may be a matter of life and death. Every moment of a stock-car race can bring drivers one step closer to victory or defeat.

Fans come for the thrill of watching expert drivers speed around the track. The sound of roaring engines fills the air. **Spectators** hear the high-speed peel of tyres at every turn.

spectator – a person who watches an event

CHAPTER 1

PILEUP AT DAYTONA

The Daytona International Speedway is one of the most important stock-car racetracks in the world. It's been the scene of many wild moments in NASCAR history, including the largest stock-car crash ever.

The year was 1960. Fans were eager for a fast race, and they got it. During the very first lap Dick Foley rounded a turn and spun out. His car went sideways across the track. The cars behind him were going at least 225 kilometres (140 miles) per hour. They tried to avoid him and went spinning off the course! Many flipped over completely.

Larry Frank was one of the 37 drivers who ended up in this record-shattering pileup. He said after the accident, "My car flipped once, became airborne and sailed completely over number 21." It was a crash he would never forget. Nor would anyone else involved. The drivers escaped with only minor injuries and a crazy story to tell.

The Daytona International Speedway stadium is more than 1.6 km (1 mile) long.

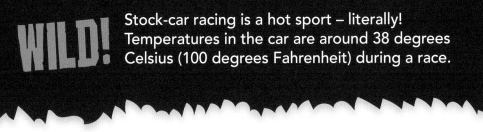

WILD! Stock-car racing is a hot sport – literally! Temperatures in the car are around 38 degrees Celsius (100 degrees Fahrenheit) during a race.

RIVALS TO THE END

There are many **rivalries** between NASCAR drivers. In 1976 two drivers took the lead in the Daytona 500. The race has 200 laps. Richard Petty and David Pearson battled for first place for 45 of them. One of the men was always in the lead during the last quarter of the race.

Competing for the lead was nothing new for Petty and Pearson. The two men had already raced against each other many times. In the 1967 season they took first and second place in 57 races. If one crossed the finish line, the other was always right behind. Petty and Pearson didn't know it, but this time the battle for first place would be very different than the races before.

rivalry – a fierce feeling of competition between two people or teams

 **WILD!** NASCAR drivers do not need a driver's licence to race. That means a driver could compete in a dangerous race, but not be allowed to drive a car home afterward.

Richard Petty and David Pearson both ended the 1976 Daytona 500 with wrecked cars.

Despite the damage done to his car, David Pearson was still able to cross the finish line.

In the third turn of the final lap Pearson passed Petty. The pass pushed Pearson ahead. But Petty stayed close. In turn four, the cars collided. Petty's car spun away, into the grass. Pearson's car slid into a pit, where it hit another car. Out in the grass, Petty's engine stopped and would not restart. This gave Pearson a clear shot to the finish line. It was only 56 metres (50 yards) ahead. Pearson's wrecked car was able to creep across the finish line at just 40 km (25 miles) per hour.

FLAGS

Flags are important in NASCAR races. They are used to communicate with drivers. The flagman sits in a stand at the finish line and waves each flag for drivers and fans to see. Each of the eight flags has a different colour and meaning.

GREEN FLAG
This is shown at the start of the race. Green means go!

YELLOW
Drivers must slow down due to a wreck or debris on the track.

RED
All cars must stop immediately when a red flag is waved. This is usually for safety reasons.

BLACK
The black consultation flag means drivers must report to officials within five laps.

BLACK FLAG WITH DIAGONAL WHITE STRIPES
If a driver ignores a black flag, they are given a warning with a black flag with white stripes.

BLUE FLAG WITH DIAGONAL YELLOW STRIPE
This courtesy flag is for drivers that should yield to faster approaching cars.

WHITE
The white flag means the lead driver has begun the final lap.

CHEQUERED FLAG
The chequered flag is every driver's favourite one to see! It is waved when the winner crosses the finish line.

CHAPTER 3

SEEING CLEARLY

Some crashes change the course of a driver's career. Some can even change the sport itself. In 1984 Ricky Rudd entered the Busch Clash. He was going into a turn when his car suddenly went sideways. The wheels caught on the side of the track. The front of his car went skyward. His car spun across the grass and flipped upside down in the air. It came to rest on all four wheels.

Rudd walked away with his eyes swollen shut. He went on to race the very next week. It was a dangerous choice. NASCAR wanted to prevent such dangerous choices in the future. After his accident, NASCAR **implemented** a rule that drivers must be examined by a doctor after every crash before they can race again.

implement – to put into practice

WILD! President Ronald Reagan was the first US president to go to a NASCAR race. He attended the 1984 Daytona 500. After the race he ate fried chicken at a picnic with the drivers and teams.

Stock-cars have a number painted on the sides and the top of the car. This helps fans keep track of the car as it races, or during a wild wreck.

CHAPTER 4

PASS IN THE GRASS

It is important for all drivers to watch for crashes, so they can avoid joining a pileup.

WILD!

Today, NASCAR's top points winner earns the Sprint Cup. This prize has had several names. It was originally called the Grand National. From 1972 to 2003 it was called the Winston Cup. From 2004 to 2007 it was named the Nextel Cup.

Every lap in a stock race is important. But no lap is as important as the final one.

The 1987 Winston All-Star Race began with a lineup of NASCAR greats. Bill Elliott emerged early on as a leader in the pack. He won 121 of 135 laps. Dale Earnhardt was close behind the entire time. In the last 10 laps, Earnhardt overtook Elliott. The cars bumped together as they fought for first place.

Bill Elliott was inducted into the NASCAR Hall of Fame in 2015.

As they headed into the final laps, Earnhardt unexpectedly spun out into the **infield** grass. He proved his skill as he kept his car under control. He pulled out ahead of Elliott in what is now known as the "pass in the grass".

Elliott was angry after the race. "That was probably the maddest I've ever been, but you just have to deal with it and go on," he said during an interview years later.

infield – a grassy area in the center of a race track oval

CHAPTER 5

FLYING HIGH

Fans have described stock-car racing as cars flying around the track. This doesn't mean cars actually leave the ground. But sometimes speed and a sharp turn can cause a stock-car to take flight.

This can happen if one car hits another. It can also happen with the sheer force of a fast turn. It is a reminder that during a stock-car race, anything can happen.

WILD! Racing can be expensive. The entry and inspection fee for every car entered is about £3,450 (US$4,300). The fee must be paid for both a driver's primary car and any backup cars.

After a crash, photos and videos can help drivers and teams figure out what happened and how to prevent future crashes.

Approximately 135,000 people attended the Daytona 500 on 14 February 1993.

No one who saw Rusty Wallace in the 1993 Daytona 500 will ever forget the moment he left the ground. It was a rare and wild crash. He was **manoeuvring** for position among the pack. Without touching another car, he lost control of his Ford Thunderbird. The car began to spin across the track. Then his car flipped as it rose off the track. It turned over as it flew. Long pieces of metal came apart as the car rolled to a stop on the grass. Fans worried that Wallace would be hurt. Some considered it a miracle that he suffered no major injuries. His car, however, was a complete loss.

manoeuvre – to make planned and controlled movements that require practised skills

WOMEN IN RACING

In the 1970s Janet Guthrie became the first woman to race in both the Daytona 500 and the Indianapolis 500. Many racing fans at the time were not happy to see a woman compete. Their protests did not stop her racing. She competed in 33 NASCAR premier series races during her career. Today she is considered a pioneer in stock-car racing. She was **inducted** into the International Motorsports Hall of Fame in 2006.

induct – to formally admit someone into a position or place of honour

CHAPTER 6

INFIELD BARREL ROLL

Enthusiasm for stock-car racing can be found in many countries, including Australia. In the 1980s and 1990s Australian Stock Car Auto Racing (AUSCAR) organized races in addition to NASCAR. While the rules were similar, AUSCAR drivers sat on the right-hand side of the car. They raced clockwise around the track, compared to anticlockwise in NASCAR.

Calder Park remains the best track in Australia. In 1995, driver Graeme O'Brien experienced one of the park's worst crashes. He broke from the pack alongside a competing racer. His car was nudged to the infield. It sprang into the air, barrel-rolling high above the ground. It seemed to pause just before it hit the ground. When it did, metal and glass rained down. O'Brien suffered only a black eye. His car, however, would never return to the course.

Drivers must stay close together to win, but this often means a small turn of the wheel can end in a crash.

 NASCAR has installed SAFER barriers around the edges of nearly every track. SAFER stands for "steel and foam energy reduction". The barriers reduce the force of impact for the drivers.

CHAPTER 7

A PHOTO FINISH

The white and black chequered flag falls at the end of every NASCAR race. It is what every driver hopes to see upon crossing the finish line.

Races are often won or lost before the final lap. But sometimes there is a **sprint** right to the very end. Ricky Craven and Kurt Busch know this all too well. In the 2003 Sprint Cup race they were side by side to the very end. In one turn Craven pushed Busch so his car scraped against the wall. In the next turn Busch passed him. Craven followed close on Busch's bumper. They raced neck and neck through the last lap. Even the most eagle-eyed fans could not tell who had won. The decision went to the cameras. The verdict? Craven won the race by .002 seconds!

sprint – to move or drive fast for a short distance

WILD! Stock-cars race at more than 241 km (150 miles) per hour. The average speed is 290 km (180 miles) per hour. Sometimes cars can reach more than 322 km (200 miles) per hour.

Video technology has made it easier to determine close wins. It also lets fans have the chance to see the action again and again.

CHAPTER 8

ALL IN THE FAMILY

NASCAR can feel like a family. Fans often attend races with their families. Drivers and teams travel together and work hard to win every race. Some race car drivers inspire their own children to follow their footsteps into the sport.

For Kurt and Kyle Busch, every time they get into a stock-car they are fuelled by sibling rivalry.

Kurt Busch began racing at the age of 14 in the Dwarf Car Championships. At age 10 Kyle Busch became crew chief for his brother's Dwarf car racing team.

The brothers do not always appear in the same races, but when they do, sparks can fly. The 2007 Nextel All-Star race had a prize of US$1 million (about £803,000). Each brother had his eye on crossing the finish line to claim it. Instead, Kyle lost control of his car as Kurt tried to pass him. Kurt kept control while Kyle spun out. Kurt continued the race, but he had run out of time. The crash prevented either of the brothers from winning.

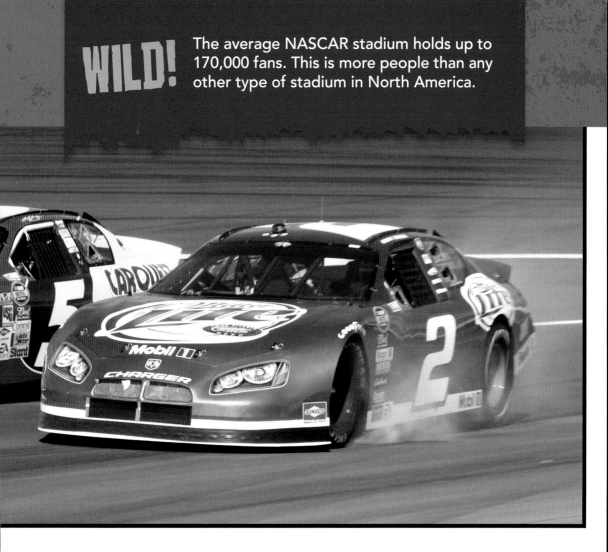

WILD! The average NASCAR stadium holds up to 170,000 fans. This is more people than any other type of stadium in North America.

"It's tough when it's for a million bucks," Kurt said after the race. The brothers were angry with each other. Their **feud** lasted until their grandmother sat them down to tell them they needed to get along. "It's just one of those moments when brothers have to test each other and neither one of us wanted to back down. In the end, it made us stronger together," Kurt said.

feud – a long-running quarrel between two people or groups of people

CHAPTER 9

NASCAR ROYALTY

Dale Earnhardt Jr drove his father's number 3 car only once. When he races, his car is number 88.

Every racer has a number painted on his or her stock-car. It helps fans identify their favourite drivers on the course.

Dale Earnhardt was one of NASCAR's greatest drivers. His number 3 was a sign that fans were in for a thrilling race. He was the son of Ralph Earnhardt, who was also a skilled stock-car driver. Dale Earnhardt died tragically during the 2001 Daytona 500. His son, Dale Earnhardt Jr, had big shoes to fill when he began his racing career.

Dale Earnhardt was a beloved NASCAR driver who earned the nickname "The Intimidator" due to his competitive driving style.

On 2 July 2010, Dale Jr did something no NASCAR driver had ever done before. He raced under his father's number. He won the race, flying past every car on the track. He raced to **honour** his late father. It was just a month after Dale Earnhardt had been inducted into the NASCAR Hall of Fame. Many fans were brought to tears by the unique and powerful moment.

honour – to give praise or show respect

CHAPTER 10

UPSIDE-DOWN NIGHT

Every stock-car race has the potential to be a driver's best race, or his worst. In the United Kingdom the British Stock Car Association (BriSCA) holds races that are known as Formula One. These races feature the greatest drivers in the UK.

Dennis "The Menace" Middler is no stranger to the danger and excitement of Formula One. In May 2016 Middler entered the second lap of a race determined to win. It is not unusual for cars to make contact in Formula One. But what happened next shocked the fans and Middler alike. After making contact with a couple of other cars, Middler's car spiralled into the air. It turned upside down, over and over again. He crashed to the ground hard. Thanks to his safety equipment, he was able to scramble from the car immediately, to the relief and joy of his fans.

He recounted the crash. "We're going pretty quick round the track and I got pushed inside a bit, climbed over the top of the other guy because we are open wheel, and it was then one of those crashes where you just close your eyes and wait."

Formula One cars are open to the air. This means there is a lot of pressure on drivers' heads and necks. They must develop strong necks to be successful racers.

GLOSSARY

feud a long-running quarrel between two people or groups of people

honour to give praise or show respect

implement to put into practice

induct to formally admit someone into a position or place of honour

infield a grassy area in the center of a race track oval

manoeuvre to make planned and controlled movements that require practised skills

rivalry a fierce feeling of competition between two people or teams

spectator a person who watches an event

sprint to move or drive fast for a short distance

FIND OUT MORE

Behind the Wheel of a Stock Car (In the Driver's Seat), Beth Bence Reinke (Child's World, 2016)

Stars of Stock Car Racing (Sports Stars), Mari Schuh (Capstone Press, 2014)

Stock Cars (Now That's Fast!), Kate Riggs (Franklin Watts, 2011)

White Lightning (Rolling Thunder Stock Car Racing), Don Keith and Kent Wright (Macmilan, 2014)

WEBSITES

http://www.accelerationnation.com/index.html

http://www.nascar.com

http://www.nascarracinggames.org/

http://www.sikids.com/

INDEX